phpMyAdmin Starter

Get started with this quick introduction to phpMyAdmin, its features, and the community

Marc Delisle

[PACKT] PUBLISHING open source community experience distilled

BIRMINGHAM - MUMBAI

phpMyAdmin Starter

First published: September 2011

Production Reference: 1050811

Published by Packt Publishing Ltd.
Livery Place
35 Livery Street
Birmingham B3 2PB, UK.

ISBN 978-1-849517-54-6

www.packtpub.com

www.PacktPub.com

Support files, eBooks, discount offers and more

You might want to visit www.PacktPub.com for support files and downloads related to your book.

Did you know that Packt offers eBook versions of every book published, with PDF and ePub files available? You can upgrade to the eBook version at www.PacktPub.com and as a print book customer, you are entitled to a discount on the eBook copy. Get in touch with us at service@packtpub.com for more details.

At www.PacktPub.com, you can also read a collection of free technical articles, sign up for a range of free newsletters and receive exclusive discounts and offers on Packt books and eBooks.

http://PacktLib.PacktPub.com

www.PacktLib.PacktPub.com

Do you need instant solutions to your IT questions? PacktLib is Packt's online digital book library. Here, you can access, read and search across Packt's entire library of books.

Why Subscribe?

- Fully searchable across every book published by Packt
- Copy and paste, print and bookmark content
- On demand and accessible via web browser

Free Access for Packt account holders

If you have an account with Packt at www.PacktPub.com, you can use this to access PacktLib today and view nine entirely free books. Simply use your login credentials for immediate access.

PACKTLIB®

Table of Contents

phpMyAdmin Starter

Welcome to the phpMyAdmin Starter. This book has been especially created to provide you with all the information that you need to get set up with phpMyAdmin. You will learn the basics of phpMyAdmin, get started with creating your own tables, and discover some tips and tricks for using phpMyAdmin.

This document contains the following sections:

So what is phpMyAdmin? – find out what phpMyAdmin actually is, what you can do with it, and why it's so great.

Installation – learn how to download and install phpMyAdmin with the minimum fuss and then set it up so that you can use it as soon as possible.

Quick start – this section will show you how to perform one of the core tasks of phpMyAdmin, creating tables. Follow the steps to create your own tables, which will be the basis of most of your work in phpMyAdmin.

Top features you need to know about – here you will learn how to perform five tasks with the most important features in phpMyAdmin. By the end of this section you will be able to browse, search, and change data, and create relations.

People and places you should get to know – every Open Source project is centered around a community. This section provides you with many useful links to the project page and forums, as well as a number of helpful articles, tutorials, blogs, and the Twitter feeds of phpMyAdmin super-contributors.

So, what is phpMyAdmin?

phpMyAdmin is a PHP application that provides a complete interface to manage MySQL databases over the Web. The following image depicts the product's home page; the main sections—MySQL and Web server—indicate that phpMyAdmin relies on a PHP-enabled web server to send commands to a MySQL server and receive data from the server:

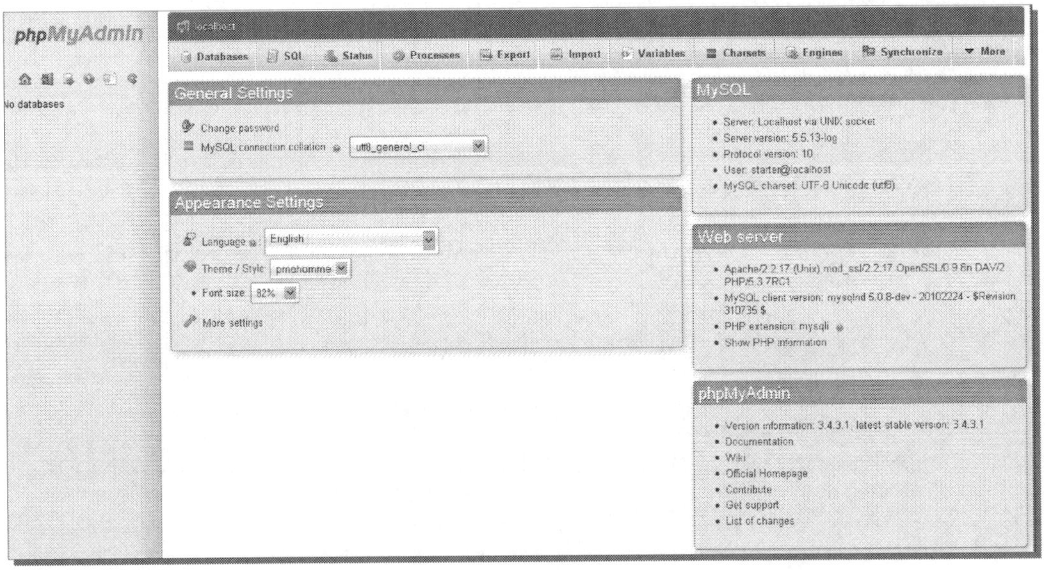

As MySQL is the database of choice on the Web and PHP is a popular web scripting language, web host providers often provide phpMyAdmin for their users as the de facto mechanism to administrate their databases.

Typical users

Users of phpMyAdmin can be broken down into these categories:

- Web developers
- Database administrators
- IT students and teachers

The authors of other web applications often advise administrators to use phpMyAdmin, either for initially populating the required database, or as a back entry in case they are locked down from their application.

Available functions

phpMyAdmin offers panels to manage the structure of data: creating, editing, deleting various elements like databases, tables, columns, indexes, views, and foreign keys (relations). The software also enables you to deal with the data itself: inserting, editing, and deleting data; sorting; searching in tables or databases; importing and exporting to various file formats.

A system administrator can also use phpMyAdmin to acquire status information about the MySQL server; this information can be used to fine-tune the server. Moreover, maintenance of MySQL usernames and privileges is available.

Advanced functions include:

- Generating system documentation, including table relations in graphical form
- Transforming data (for example to show a thumbnail of an image stored as a **BLOB** (**Binary Large Object**); see `http://dev.mysql.com/doc/refman/5.5/en/blob.html`)
- Tracking changes on structure and data
- Keeping bookmarks of frequently-used queries
- Maintaining users' preferences about phpMyAdmin's settings
- Synchronizing databases between servers

Volunteers all over the world help the development team by providing translations for the interface in many languages.

Installation

In four easy steps, you can install phpMyAdmin and get it set up on your system.

Step 1—What do I need?

Before you install phpMyAdmin, you will need to check that you have all of the required elements, as listed below:

- phpMyAdmin requires a web server environment that supports PHP, for example Apache (`http://httpd.apache.org/`) or IIS (`http://www.iis.net/`).
- 25MB free (minimum) disk space on the web server. You will require more free space to store your data in MySQL.
- phpMyAdmin is written in the PHP scripting language. phpMyAdmin v 3.4.x requires a minimum of PHP v5.2.0.0 to run.
- The minimum supported MySQL version is 5.0.x.
- You need MySQL account information (username, password)

Step 2—Downloading phpMyAdmin

The recommended way to download phpMyAdmin is as a compressed package from `http://phpmyadmin.net/`. We suggest that you download the most current stable build.

Pick a file which has an extension for which you have the corresponding extractor program. Moreover, there are packages which contain only the English message files and other packages, marked `all-languages`, which contain all supported languages. Let's suppose you downloaded `phpMyAdmin-3.4.3.1-all-languages.zip` and saved it to your local workstation.

After downloading and unpacking this archive, you will be left with a directory called `phpMyAdmin-3.4.3.1`, containing a number of files and folders.

Step 3—Configuring phpMyAdmin

The main configuration file is named `config.inc.php` and its normal location is the top-level directory (where `index.php` is located). A single instance of phpMyAdmin can manage many MySQL servers; therefore, this file can contain sections for more than one MySQL server. It can also contain directives that control the behavior of the interface. All these directives are explained in `Documentation.html`.

If this file is not found, phpMyAdmin assumes that you want to connect to a MySQL server on `localhost`—the same host as the web server. This might fit your purpose.

It's recommended to use the sample configuration file, `config.sample.inc.php`, and copy it over `config.inc.php`; then, look it over and follow the examples therein.

Step 4—Uploading to your web server

Using the uploading mechanism available on your web server, you should now place the whole folder in your web server documents directory, in which case the tool will be located at `http://yourwebserver.com/phpMyAdmin-3.4.3.1`. The exact location and URL really depends on your host's policies.

You can rename the folder; however, the final name it should bear depends on a number of factors:

- Is there more than one phpMyAdmin version installed on the server?
- Is this a multi-user installation, where users are accustomed to call it by a special URL like `http://yourwebserver.com/mysql`?

The following examples will assume that the folder was renamed to `phpMyAdmin`.

And that's it!!

By this point, you should have a working installation of phpMyAdmin and are free to play around and discover more about it.

Further configuration

Now that the folder is in place on the web server, you can use a web-based setup script to refine your configuration. The advantage of configuring this way is that all directives are conveniently regrouped by menus and submenus, such as **Features, Navigation frame, and Import.**

Visiting `http://yourwebserver.com/phpMyAdmin/setup` displays the following initial screen:

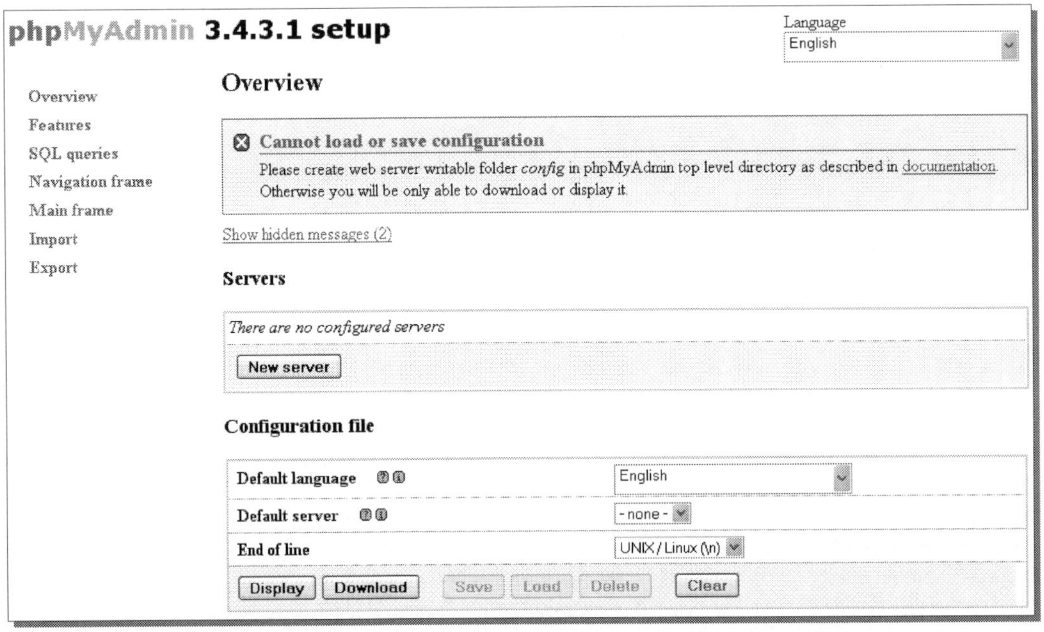

At this point, you are able to use the various menus and buttons—notably the **New server** button—to explore the configuration possibilities. You'll note that the setup script cannot currently load or save a configuration file. This is because a protection mechanism exists. If anyone could visit this URL and configure phpMyAdmin, your installation would be at risk. Therefore, you need to have access to the folder where you installed phpMyAdmin, to create a subfolder named `config` which can be used temporarily during the configuration steps. The web server itself must have the rights to write to this folder.

When this subfolder has been created, reload the page; now you can use the **Save** button and this creates a `config.inc.php` under the `config` subfolder.

After configuration is done, you need to do the following:

- Copy the newly created `config.inc.php` to the top-level directory—this makes it the effective configuration.
- Change the permissions on the copied `config.inc.php` to ensure that the web server cannot write to it.
- Delete the `config` directory (or at least change its permissions to avoid any writing in it)

Quick start—Creating your first tables

phpMyAdmin is all about managing MySQL tables, so this section guides you in creating a database to hold your new project, then creating two tables.

The theme for the sample tables is a grocery store, with departments and items. Of course an information system for a real grocery store would contain many more tables describing employees, suppliers, and sales but two tables will suffice for our purpose.

We suppose here that your MySQL username is `sarah` and that this account is allowed to create databases with the prefix `sarah_`.

Step 1—Creating a database

A MySQL database is a container for tables. The new database will be named `sarah_grocery`, assuming that the system administrator enforces the policy that all databases must have the username as a prefix. The rest of the database name consists of the project name, which here is `grocery`.

Currently you might be seeing one existing database, `information_schema`. This is not a real database but contains metadata about the whole data structure.

1. Log in to MySQL via phpMyadmin's login panel, with the username **sarah**.
2. Click on the **Databases** menu tab.
3. Change the database name from **sarah_...** to **sarah_grocery**.
4. Click on the **Create** button.

Step 2—Opening the database

You must now tell phpMyAdmin to use **sarah_grocery** as the current database. This way, all actions will take place in the context of this database. The easiest way to open it is by clicking on the database name from the navigation panel (which is located on the left-hand side if you are using a left-to-right language like English).

Step 3—Creating the first table

Now that you have a database to play with, it's time to create a table that will hold the description of the grocery's departments. To be able to create inter-table relations in a later task without the need for installing further phpMyAdmin elements, all the tables in this exercise will use the InnoDB storage engine—see `http://www.innodb.com` and `http://dev.mysql.com/doc/refman/5.5/en/innodb-storage-engine.html`.

InnoDB is a good choice for the storage engine, as it offers solid performance, transactions, referential integrity, and crash recovery.

When opening a database, you are by default in its **Structure** page where you can see existing tables and views belonging to this database. You now use the **Create table** initial dialog to specify the table name and initial number of columns:

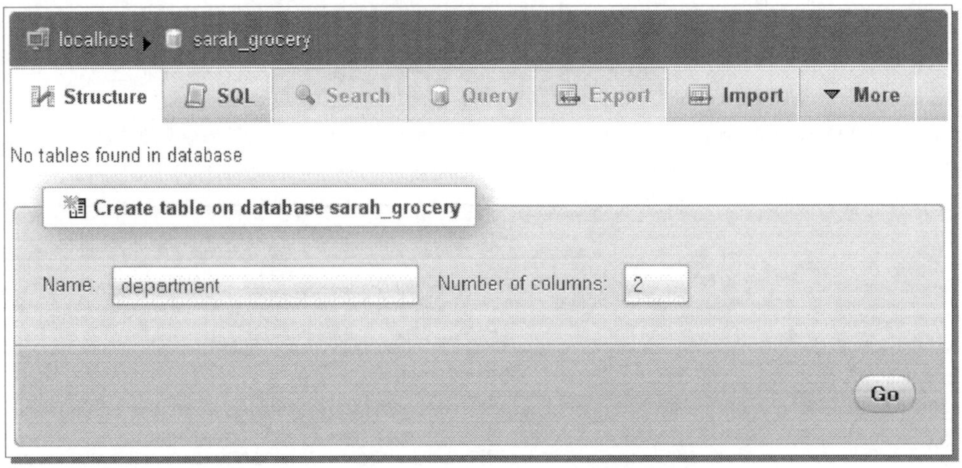

Clicking on **Go** brings up the columns panel where you'll create two columns, `id` (an integer column) and `description` (a variable-size character column having a maximum length of 100). The `id` column is marked as being the primary key.

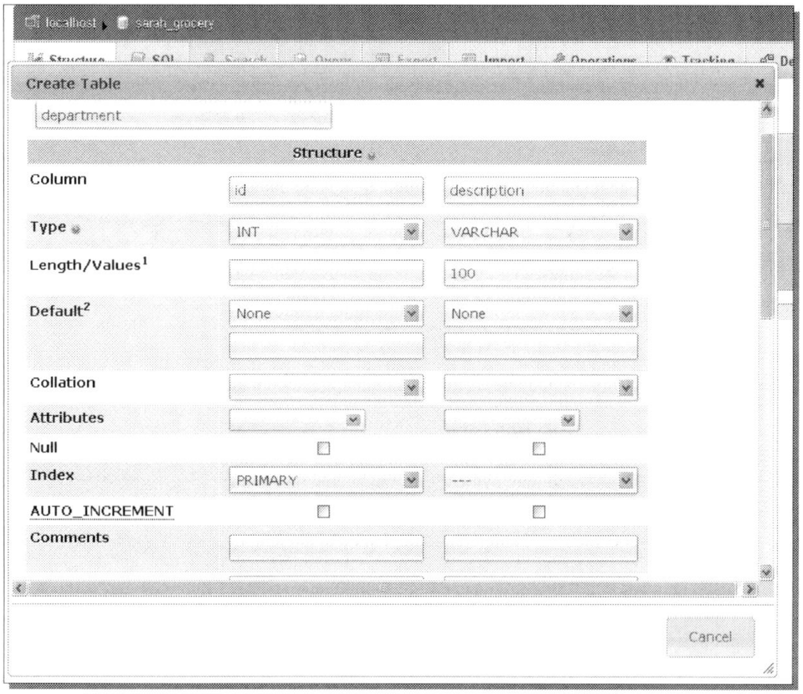

Scrolling to the bottom of this panel and clicking **Save** creates the table. You now see a different **Structure** panel, which shows the existing table, **department**, on which you can apply actions, and the **Create table** dialog to create further tables.

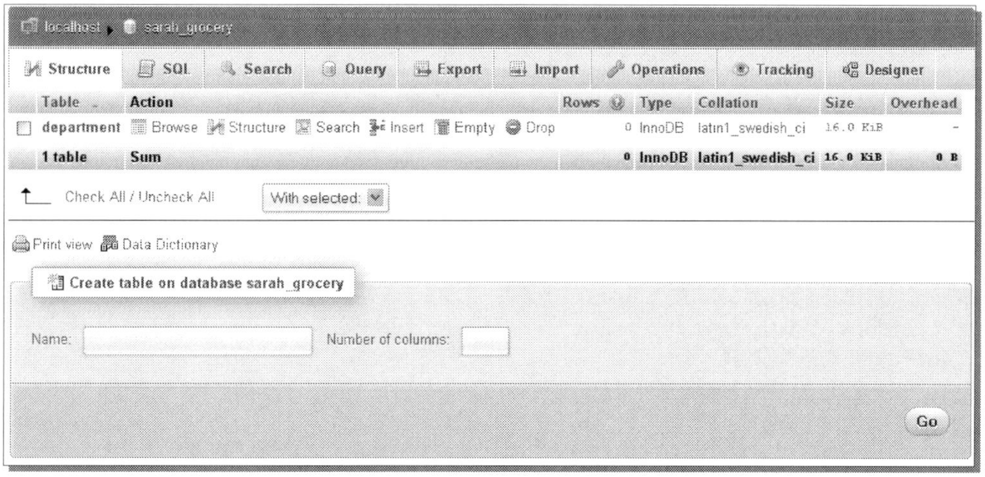

Step 4—Creating the second table

You will now use your table creation skills to create the `item` table, containing the following columns:

- **id** (an integer and primary key)
- **dept_id** (an integer)
- **description** (VARCHAR 100)
- **weight** (an integer)

You will notice that both tables have a column `id` as the primary key; however, there is no risk of confusion because SQL requires using the table name in queries, such as the following:

```
SELECT id FROM item
```

Step 5—Populating the tables

You need some sample data to play with these tables. There is more than one way of inserting data into a table:

- An application that programmatically inserts data
- An `INSERT` query typed in phpMyAdmin's query box
- An import operation via phpMyAdmin's **Import** menu
- An insertion via phpMyAdmin's **Insert** menu

In the current step you'll use the **Insert** menu, which can be reached from the database **Structure** page. Let's begin by inserting new departments; on the line for the department table, click on **Insert**, which brings the insertion panel. Then enter this sample data:

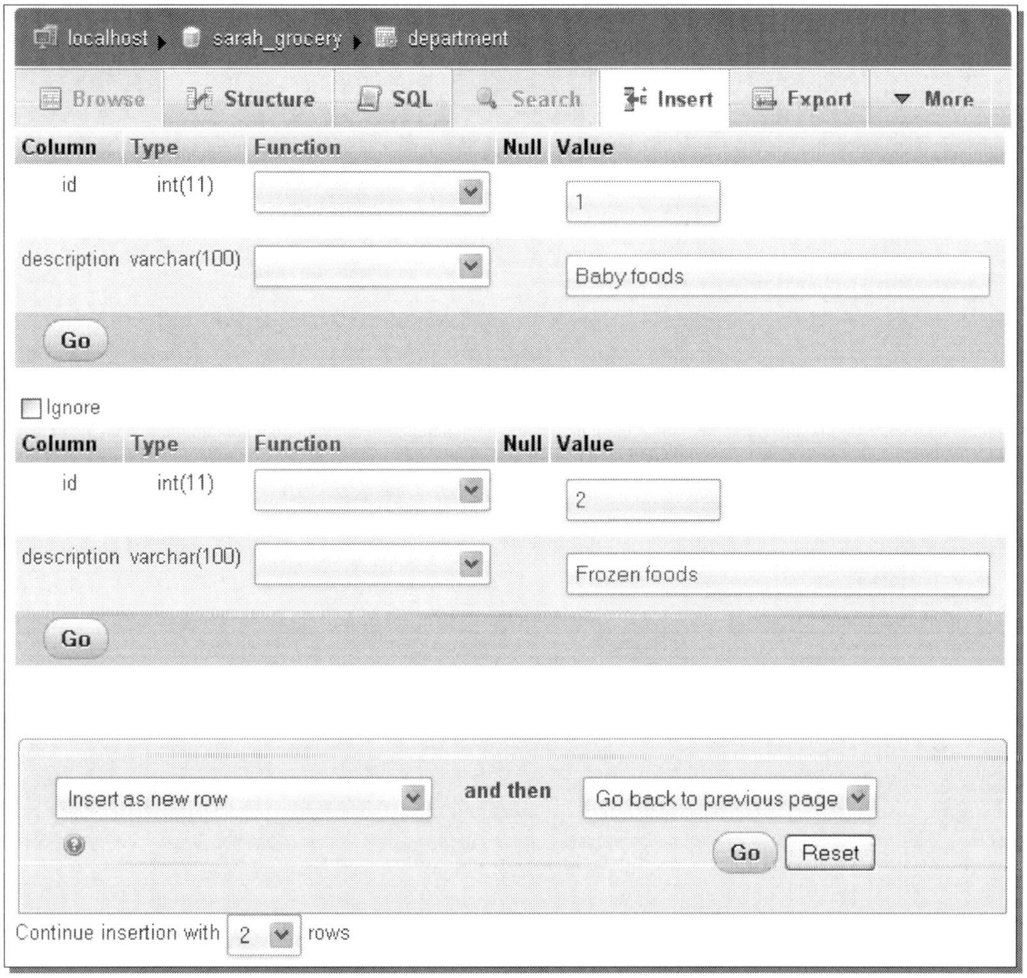

Clicking on **Go** generates the following query, sends it to the MySQL server and displays it on-screen—this is handy, both to reassure you about the action done and possibly to teach you SQL.

```
INSERT INTO `sarah_grocery`.`department` (`id` ,`description`
)
VALUES (
'1', 'Baby foods'
```

```
), (
'2', 'Frozen foods'
);
```

You need to also populate the `item` table. Here you create two items in the frozen foods department:

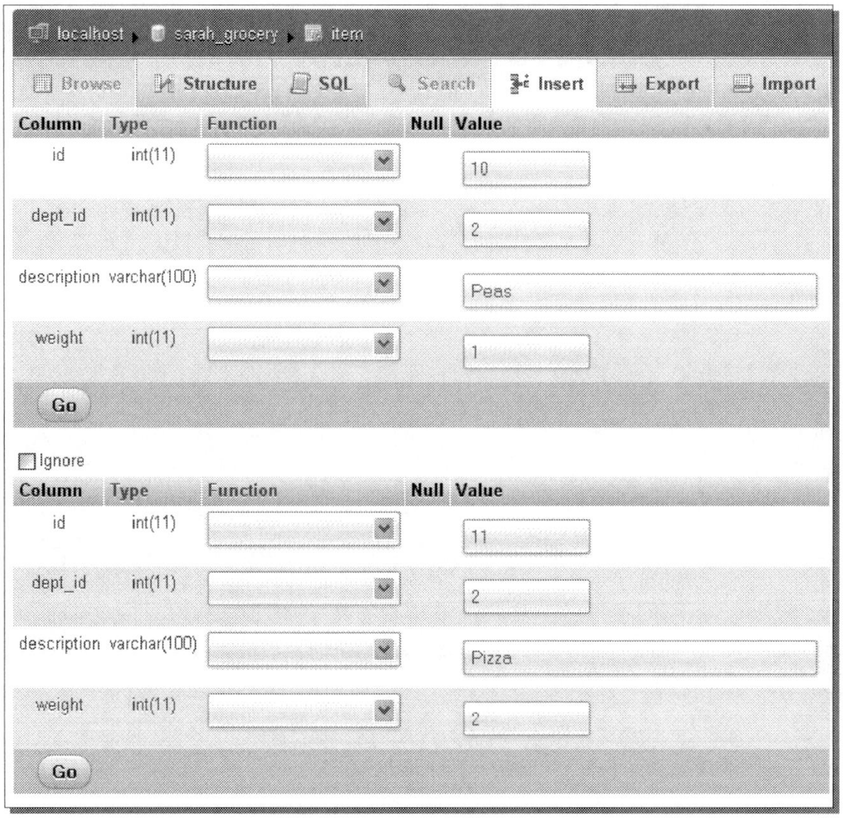

Top tasks you'll want to know about

As you start to use phpMyAdmin, you will realize that there are a wide variety of things that you can do with it. This section will show you the most commonly performed tasks in phpMyAdmin and how to do them.

Task 1—Browsing data

Probably the most common usage of phpMyAdmin is to look at data. In fact, this is so common that the default action when clicking on a table name in the navigation panel is to browse this table.

Let's see what appears when you click on the department table from the navigation (left) panel:

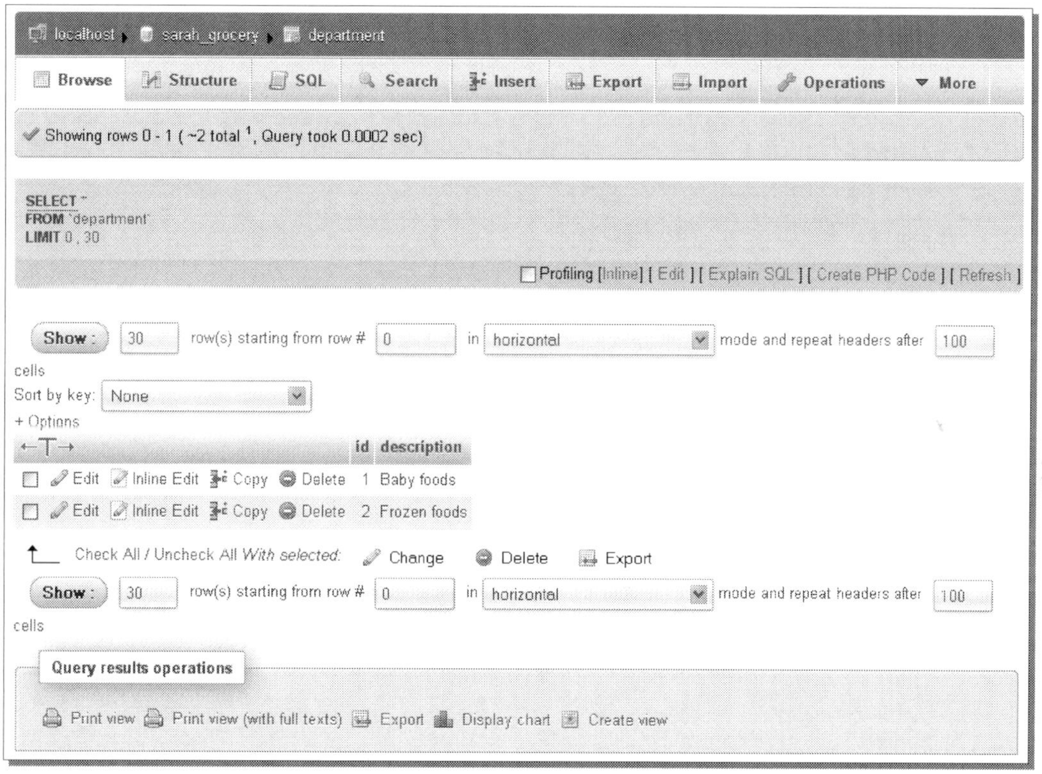

The screen in browse mode can be broken down into various sections, which are explained here, from top to bottom:

- The server / database / table locator
- The table menu, with **Browse** being highlighted
- The **Showing rows** line, indicating which rows you are looking at (first row being numbered 0) and the total number of rows
- The generated query **SELECT * FROM `department` LIMIT 0,30**
- A navigation line, from which you could specify how many rows you want and the starting row
- A **Sort by key** selector, containing all the indexes for this table from which to choose to sort
- An **Options** link (more on this below)
- A big T that enables you to show the full text of lengthy columns
- The names of the columns (clickable to sort on each column)
- The data lines, prefixed with checkbox action links **Edit, Inline Edit, Copy,** and **Delete**
- A **With selected** line, permitting to perform global actions on the lines for which the corresponding checkbox has been marked
- The **Query results operations** section, from which you can generate a **Print view** of the table, **Export** the results, or generate a chart from the data

Clicking on **Options** opens a sliding section, offering you more ways of displaying the data for BLOB columns, binary columns, or relational information:

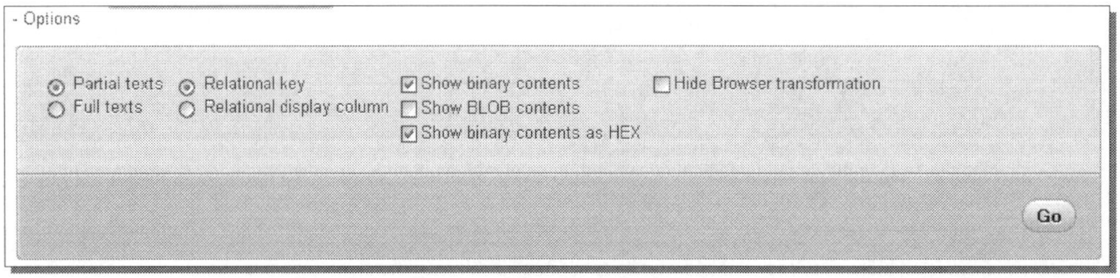

Browsing is not just looking at raw data; phpMyAdmin can also sort this data. Sorting can be performed on an index, using the **Sort by key** selector, or simply by clicking on a column header. Clicking again on the same header reverses the sort. You can experiment now by clicking twice on the **description** header.

When there are numerous rows of data, they are presented by pages and you can navigate back and forth between these pages. Here is an example of navigation controls with a different table, taken from MySQL's sakila database (`http://dev.mysql.com/doc/sakila/en/sakila.html`):

Task 2—Searching data

For small tables like your `department` and `item` tables, it's often sufficient to browse them in order to grasp all their data. However, for larger projects involving many tables or many data rows, you have to rely on phpMyAdmin's search mechanisms.

You can search on a single table or on many tables at once. Let's begin by examining the single-table case, using the `item` table.

You can enter the table **Search** page with either of these methods:

- Opening the `sarah_grocery` database on its **Structure** page and clicking the **Search** link on the line corresponding to the **item** table
- Opening the **item** table and clicking the **Search** menu tab

The initial search page looks like the following, with only the most commonly-used **"query by example"** section visible:

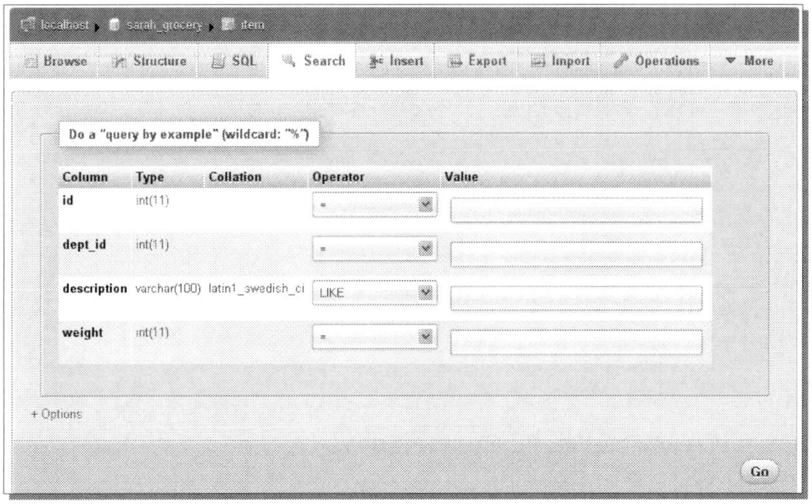

In a query by example search, you fill one or more values corresponding to what you are looking for. You can also apply an operator to a value in order to modify the search behavior.

Let's search for some pizza; for this, you simply enter **pizza** (with a lowercase **p**) in the value field next to the **description**; then you click on **Go**, which brings the following results screen:

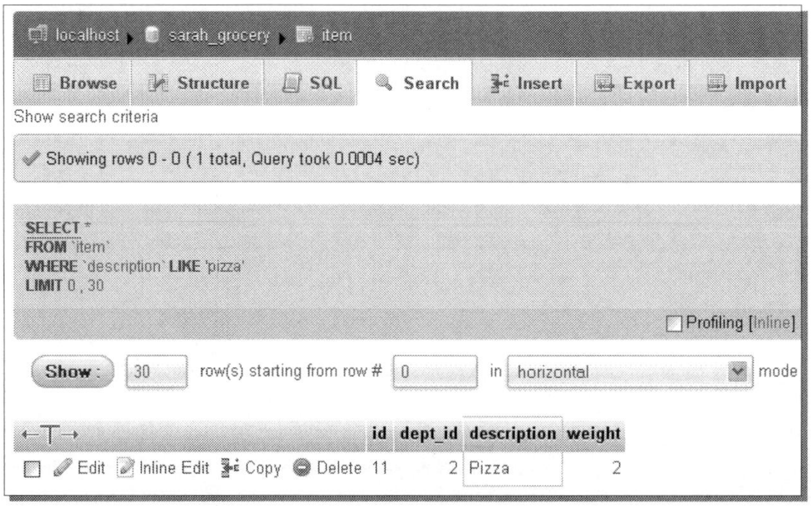

A few remarks about this screen:

- We entered **pizza** but MySQL found **Pizza**; this is because the `description` column uses one of the case-insensitive collations (`latin1_swedish_ci`, where `ci` means case-insensitive)
- The **description** column in the results is highlighted with a colored border
- We are now in a normal results panel and all the possibilities related to browsing are available (page navigation, sorting, and so on)
- The search criteria panel has been hidden but can be brought back using the **Show search criteria** link located just under the menu tabs

To practice using a search operator:

1. Click on **Show search criteria**.
2. Enter **10** as a value for **id**.
3. Change the operator on the **id** column, to less than (**<**).
4. Click on **Go**.

No item with a `description` of Pizza and an `id` less than 10 exists, so you get the **MySQL returned an empty result set (i.e. zero rows)** message.

The search **Options** slider contains controls to restrict which columns will appear in the results, to ask for distinct results, to type in a `WHERE` clause, to specify the number of rows per page and to choose the display order.

Now you'll have a look at the multi-table (or database) search mechanism. This searching method is handy when you are not sure of the exact table that holds a piece of data you are looking for, or when the same piece of data (say, a city name) appears in more than one table or more than one column.

Opening your database and clicking on **Search** brings the database search panel. You'll first try an exact search for the number 1, in all tables. To accomplish this search:

1. Enter **1** as the value to search.
2. Tick the radio button next to **the exact phrase**.
3. Click **Select All** to pick all tables.
4. Click on **Go**.

The following image depicts the search panel just before launching the search:

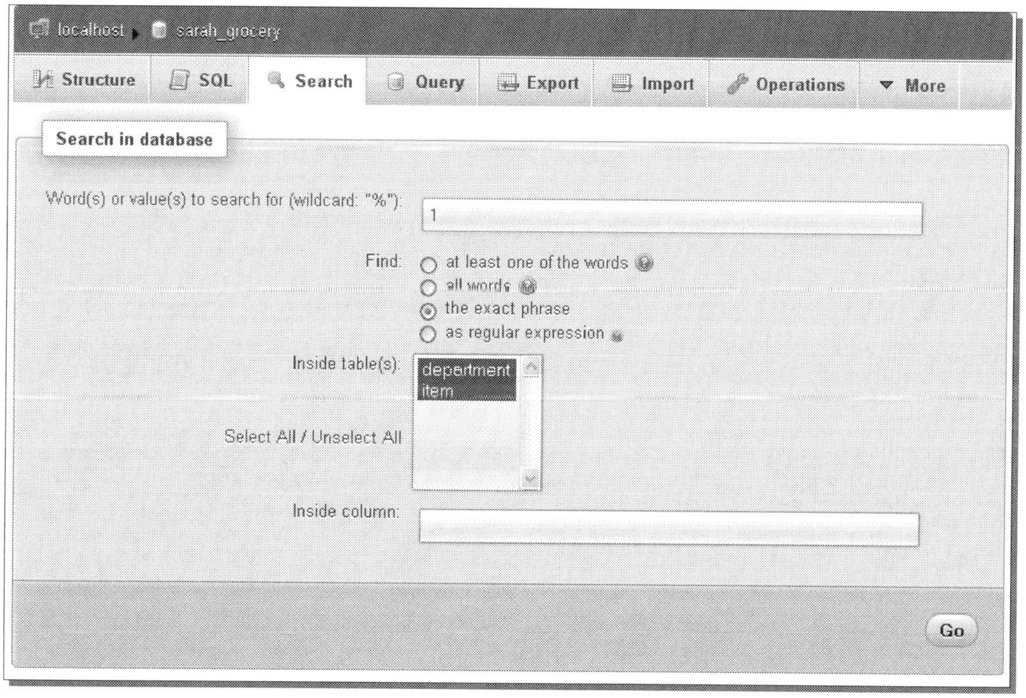

The search results first give an overview of the number of matches for each table, as well as links to browse or delete these matches:

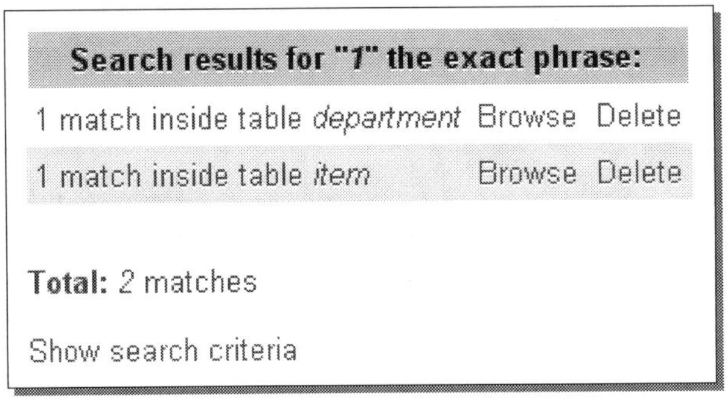

Clicking on **Browse** fetches the search results for a particular table, while leaving the global search results on the top of screen.

Note that the **Show search criteria** link is available. You now click on this link and change the search mode (in the **Find** dialog) from **the exact phrase** to **at least one of the words**. Clicking on **Go** shows different global search results with two matches inside the **item** table. The reason for this is the addition of the wildcard `%` character before and after the searched value in the generated query, which now matches the id 10 and 11 of the **item** table when looking for the number 1.

Task 3—Changing data and structure

Heraclitus, a Greek philosopher (and probably database designer precursor) told us that "Nothing is permanent except change". In the database world, not only data values often change but also their supporting structures (column, table, view, and database definitions).

You'll first explore the three graphical methods for editing data, and then you'll go on about changing data structure.

When you have a results page (generated by either browsing a table or searching in it), you notice that for each data row, **Edit** and **Inline Edit** links are offered. Moreover, a checkbox appears for each line, permitting you to choose the rows to edit via the **Change** link underneath.

Let's try the **Edit** link for the **item** table. Browsing this table and clicking on **Edit** for **id 10** brings this row in edit mode. Here you have changed the **weight** value from 1 to 3 and are about to click on **Go** to save the change:

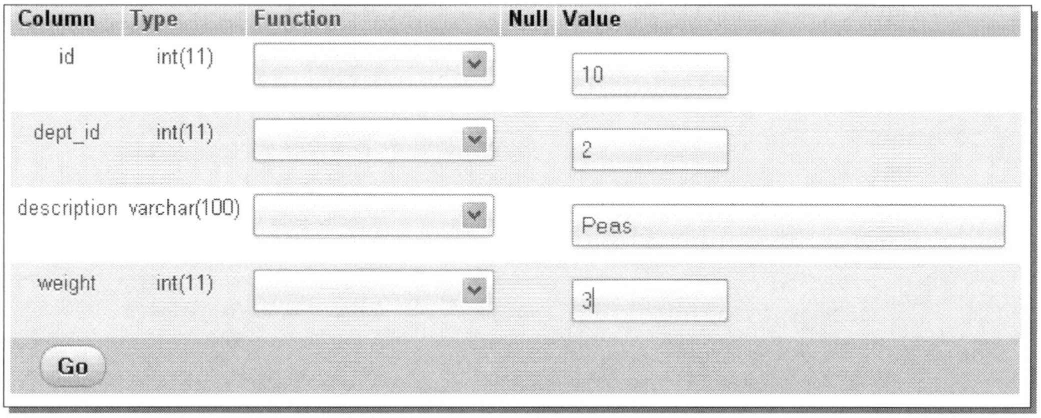

This is the most traditional mechanism to edit a row. Using the checkboxes and the **With selected: Change** link permits you to put more than one row in the edit mode at once. Here are some reasons why you might want to do this:

- To compare data from one row to another while editing
- To copy and paste data from one row to another (for example, exchanging the weight value between peas and pizzas)

More recently (in phpMyAdmin 3.4.x), inline editing was made available. Trying it for **id 10** brings you this screen:

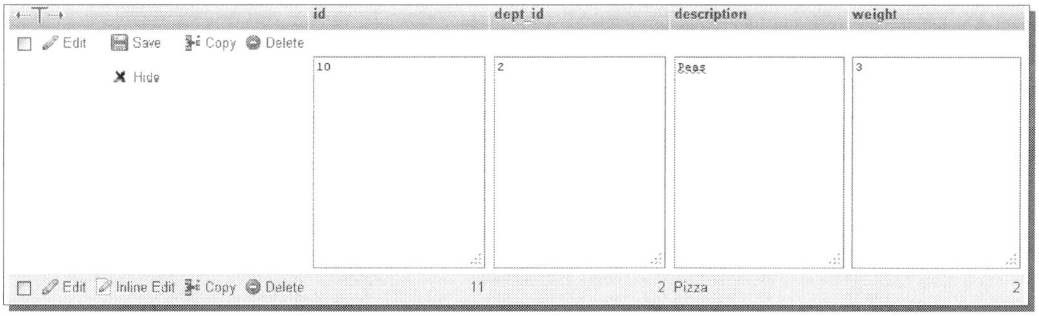

The advantage is that you did not leave the results page you were on; thus you can keep an eye on the data for the other rows, which can help you decide about the changes to make.

Directly make your changes and click on **Save**, or decide to **Hide** the inline edit view, therefore not saving any changes you made.

We will now explore how to modify the structure of data. You begin by opening the **department** table in **Structure** mode—this can be done either by clicking **Structure** for this table, or by clicking the small icon next to this table name in the navigation panel.

The **Structure** page shows you a great deal of information:

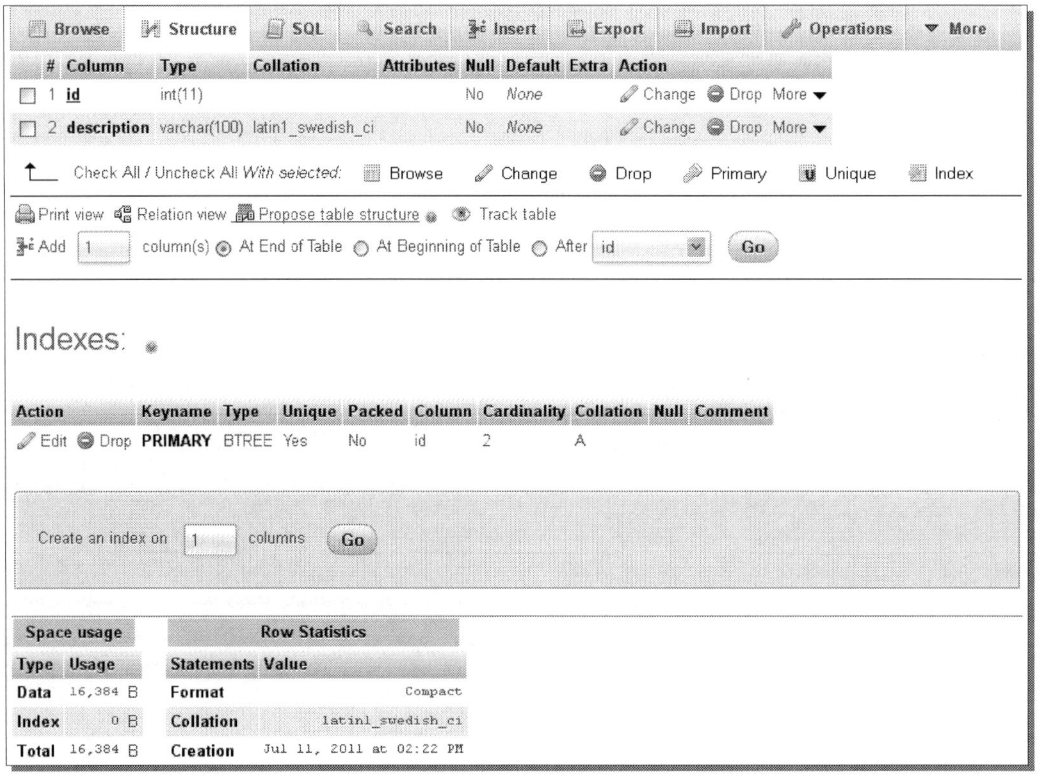

You can see three main sections:

- The list of current columns, with a dialog to add more
- The **Indexes** section, where you can edit or drop an index
- The statistics about space usage and rows

In the next exercise you will add a column that will be used to record the date of the last inspection for this department. In the dialog **Add X column(s)** you see that the default is to add one column at the end of the table; then just click on **Go,** bringing up the following panel in which you type the new column's information:

Clicking on **Save** adds this column to your table. You can now browse the **department** table and notice that there is a new column, **last_inspection,** with all the dates set to **0000-00-00** as we did not set any default date.

Editing an existing row shows you a new icon: a small calendar. Clicking on it gives you a standard date picker, shown as follows:

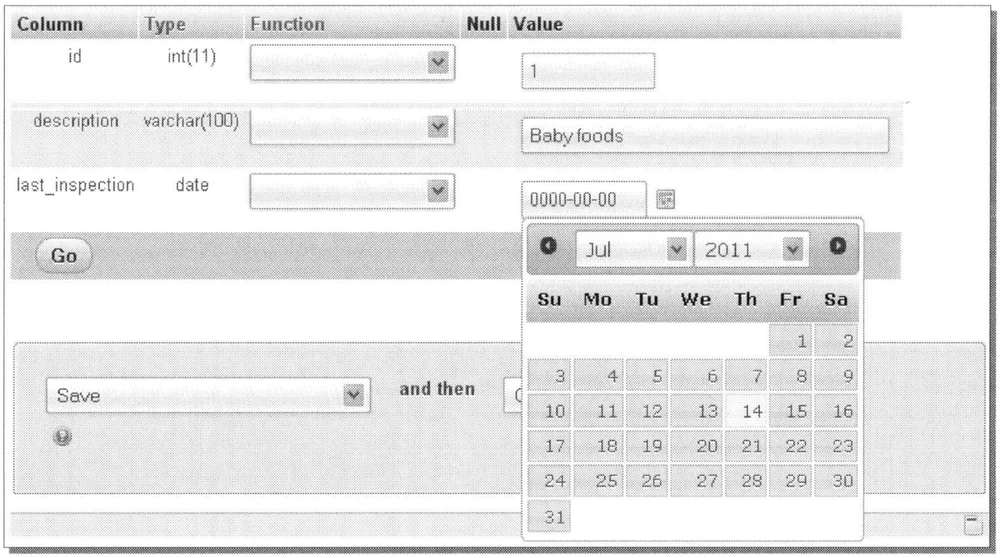

You can also change an existing column's structure—for example, the description column becoming a `VARCHAR(110)`—but beware of the consequences, should you change the type or size of the column. Data truncation could happen.

Adding an index on the **last_inspection** column can be done quickly via the **More** menu that is offered for each column:

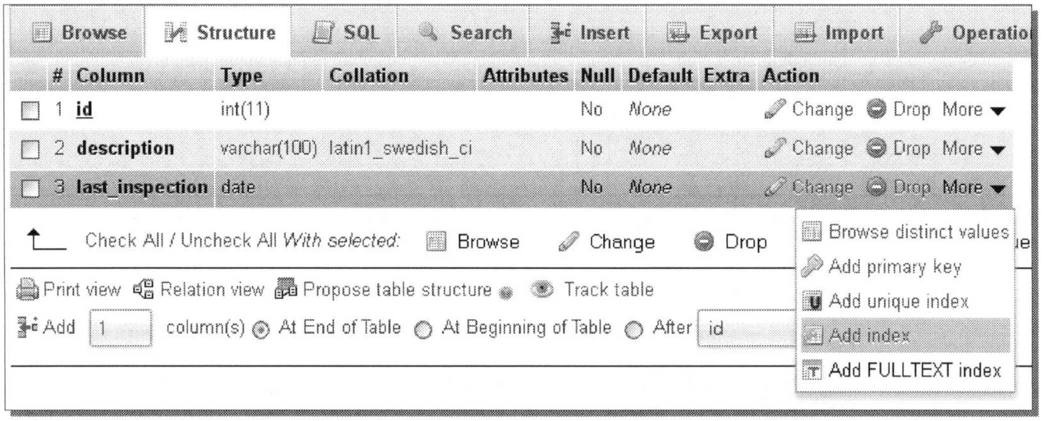

Fine-tuning indexes is accomplished via the **Indexes** section by using the **Edit** link for a specific index. Here you can add or remove columns from an index, or even change the number of characters a column uses in this index.

Task 4—Exporting to Excel

The popularity of Excel means that many people are familiar with this tool and they prefer to do the majority of their data manipulations in it. This task will describe extracting data with the goal of reading it back into Microsoft Excel. Note that any utility that understands the CSV (comma-separated values) format can be used to read the file generated in this task.

You'll first practice exporting in quick mode, and then you'll go through the custom mode for additional options.

Start by opening the **department** table and clicking **Export,** which brings up this panel:

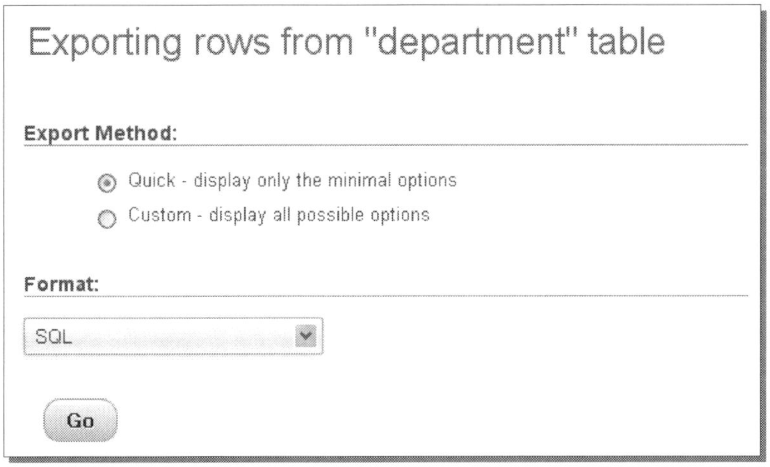

As can be seen, the default export format is **SQL** because it permits you to quickly produce a complete backup of the table's structure and data. However for this task, you need to change the export format to CSV for MS Excel.

A pure CSV file should use **Comma-Separated Values**; however as Excel uses semicolons to delineate each value, phpMyAdmin produces a file containing semicolons. You can try this format by choosing it in the **Format** selector and clicking **Go**. Your browser offers to save the file or to open it with the default program associated with `.csv` files (depending on your workstation's OS). Here is what you can see after opening the file with Excel:

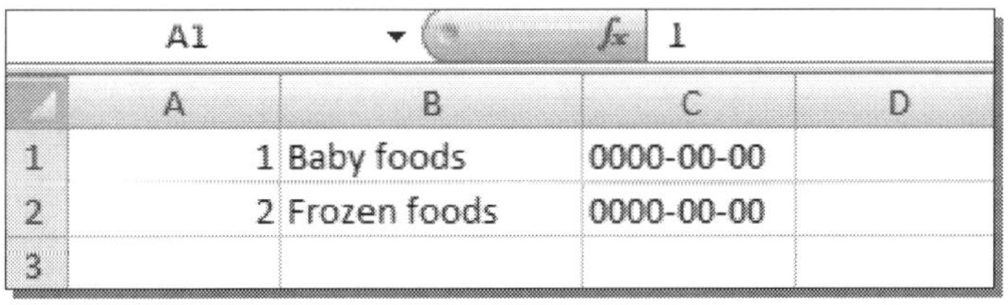

Note that in this quick export format, the column names do not appear; you'll use the custom format to remediate to this.

Contrary to the quick export format, the custom one offers many options. Some of these options (**Rows, Output**) are common for all export formats and some are adapted for each format.

Selecting **CSV for MS Excel,** and then choosing **Custom** produces the following panel:

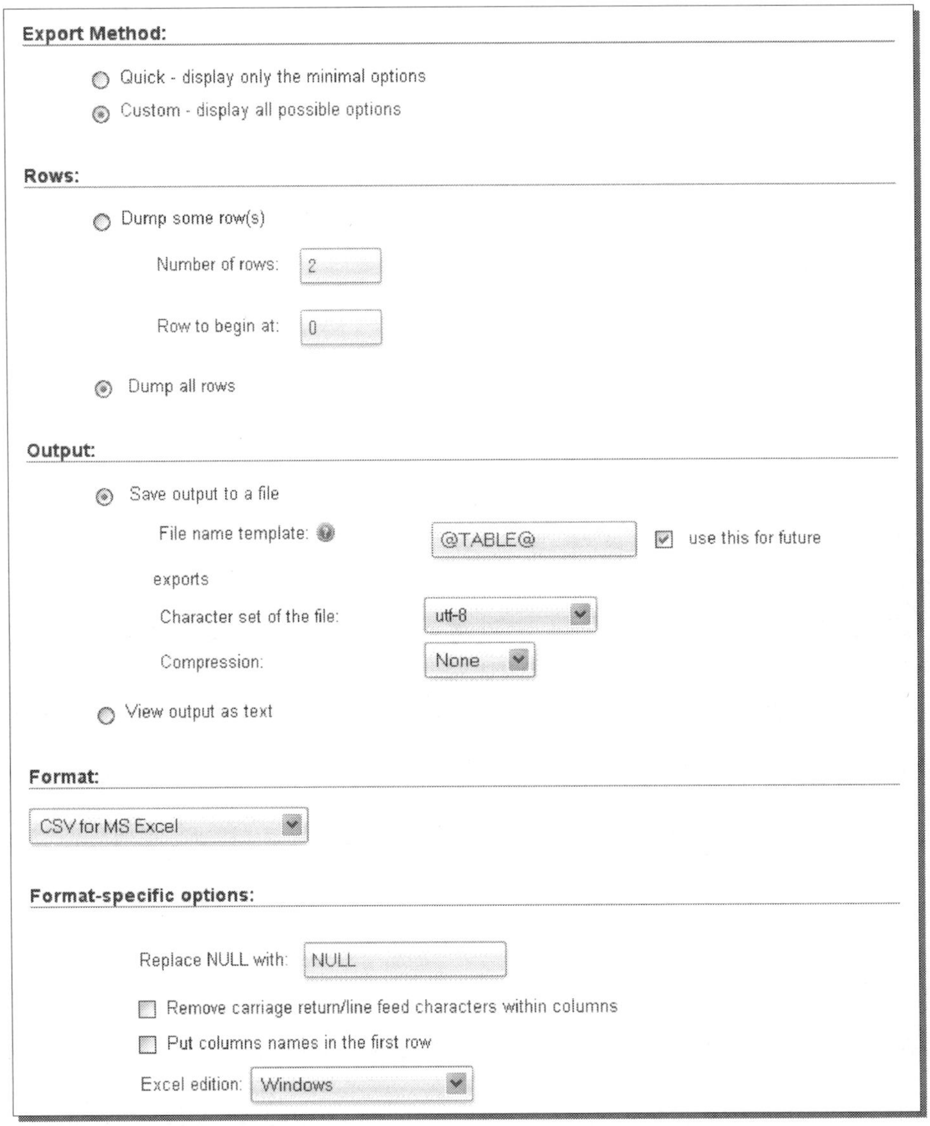

The **Rows** section enables you to choose to **Dump** (export) just some rows (with the number of rows and starting row) or all rows.

The **Output** section permits you to either save output to a file (with a choice of character set and compression) or to view the output as text (which would not save anything but can be useful in case the output format can be interpreted as text – this happens to work with the CSV format).

Next, the format-specific options vary according to the chosen format. Here, the option most likely to be changed would be **Put column names in the first row**. This would help the person opening the CSV file in Excel to see column headers indicating the original column names.

There is also a selector to pick up which **Excel edition** is the target for this file (Windows, Mac).

Task 5—Creating relations

Making relations between tables is very useful. Let's just consider the benefits of defining relations when manipulating tables via phpMyAdmin:

- The possibility of choosing the values of one column, based on a related table
- A clearer description of the relations between tables
- The possibility of generating a schema of the relations

The native way in MySQL to define relations is via the `FOREIGN KEY` constraints (more details at `http://dev.mysql.com/doc/refman/5.5/en/innodb-foreign-key-constraints.html`). These constraints are available with the InnoDB storage engine; this is why we created our tables under this engine.

In this task, you'll begin with exploring what can be done with relations using just what MySQL offers natively; then you'll learn the additional possibilities offered by phpMyAdmin, thanks to its configuration storage mechanism.

The goal here is to make a relation between the `dept_id` column of the `item` table and the `id` column of the `department` table; this is because a department should exist before you use it in the `item` table. In InnoDB vocabulary, the foreign key for `item.dept_id` will be `department.id`.

You first open the **item** table on its **Structure** page and then click on **Relation view**. This produces the following panel:

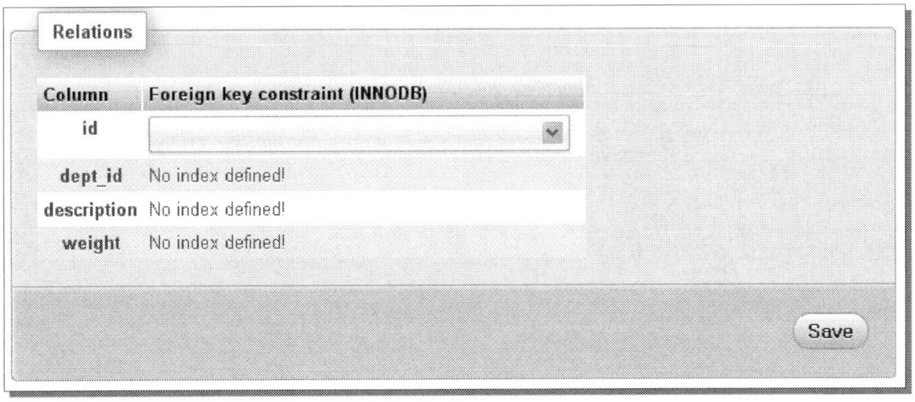

InnoDB requires that all columns referring to a foreign key or referred to as a foreign key, have an index defined. So you must go back to the **Structure** page for **item** and, for the **dept_id** column, use the **More** selector and choose **Add index**:

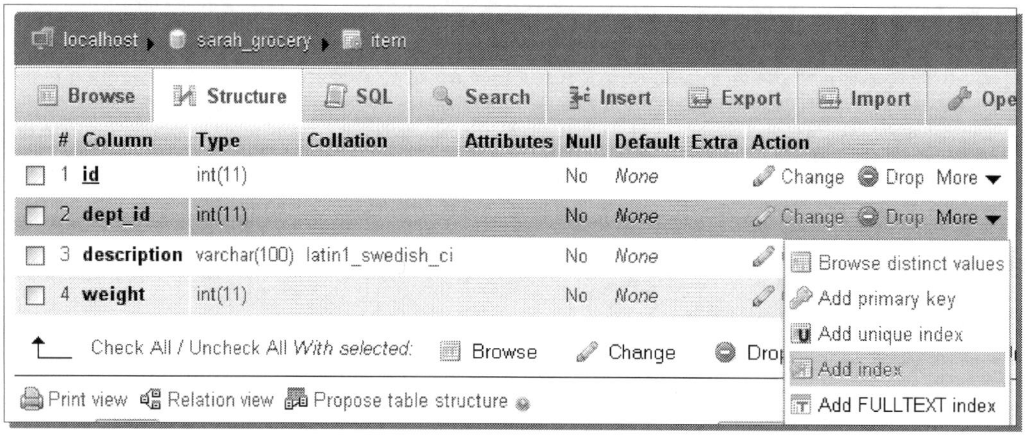

Going back to the **Relation view,** you can now choose for **dept_id** the appropriate column **department.id**. Choosing it makes other selectors appear as well:

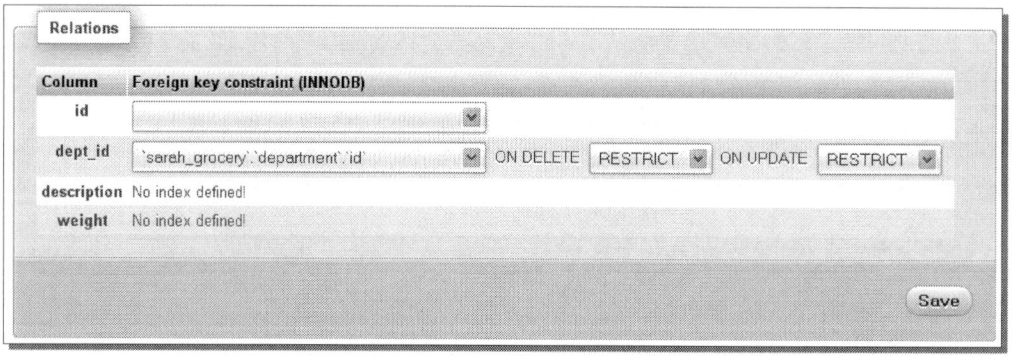

The **ON DELETE** and **ON UPDATE** are foreign key options; they are explained in the aforementioned MySQL documentation page. For now you'll just keep the default values and click on **Save**.

At this point, everything went fine because your data respected the constraint (department IDs existed in the department table).

You can immediately see a benefit of the relation by trying to **Insert** a new item; the possible department IDs appear in a drop-down selector:

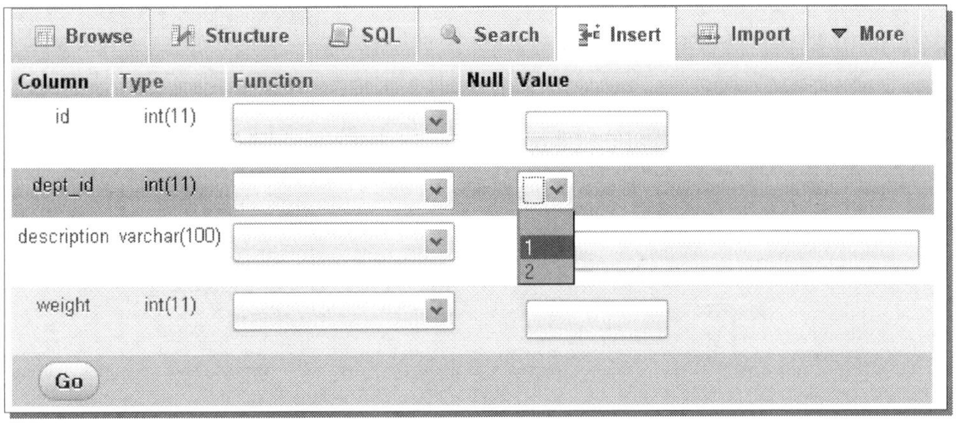

More options can be made available if your installation has the phpMyAdmin configuration storage deployed. In short, this is a special set of tables that contain metadata about various configuration elements. For example, we would like to see the department name in the drop-down selector, when we insert or edit an item. Thus, the metadata called `display column` is offered in the phpMyAdmin configuration storage, to hold which column best describes each row. Details about installing the configuration storage appear in `Documentation.html`. The remaining segments of this task assume that the configuration storage has been installed.

With this in place, you can open the **department** table in **Structure** page, click **Relation view**, and pick the column to display, which is **description**:

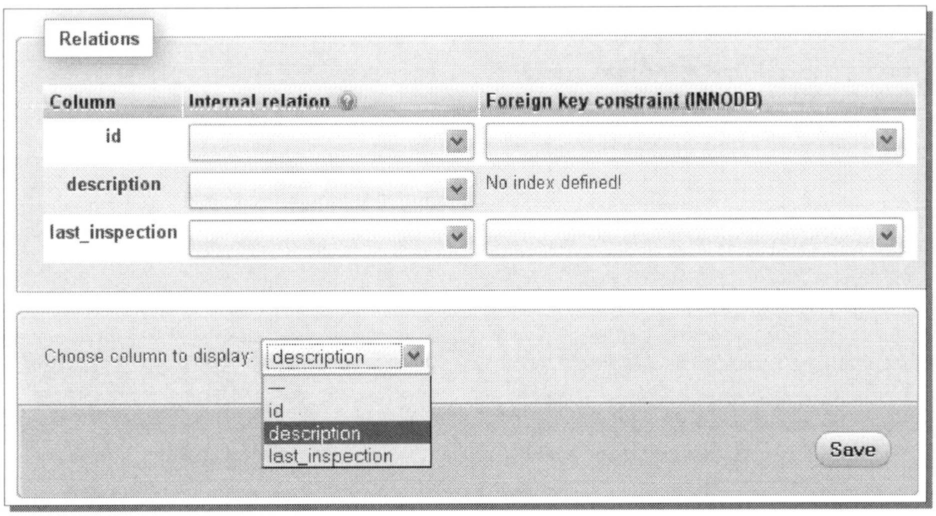

After clicking on **Save**, you can now open the **item** table in **Insert** mode and see the difference, shown as follows:

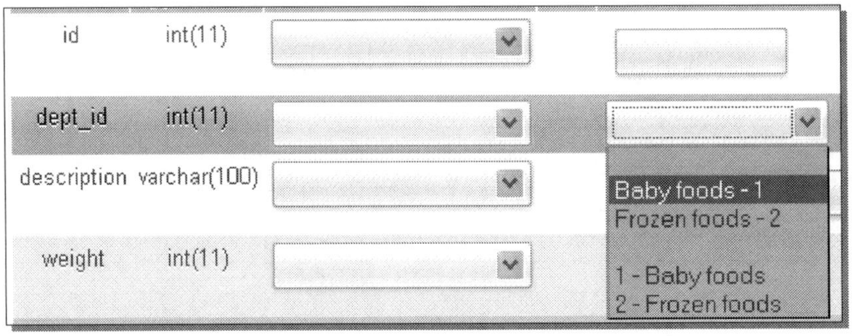

If too many rows were present in the referenced table, an icon would be offered instead of a drop-down. This icon would open a distinct panel to select among the values, with pagination and search capabilities.

Another handy feature made available by the configuration storage is the Designer. In this panel, available from the database menu, you can define the relations graphically, move the tables around on the workspace, and save their coordinates in order to produce a PDF schema of the relations. The following is an image of the Designer's workspace:

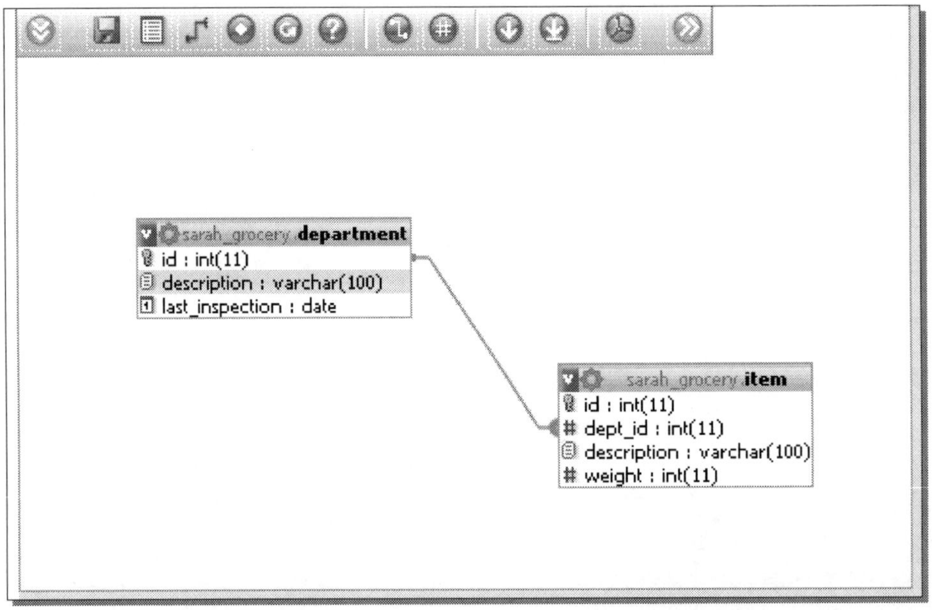

People and places you should get to know

If you need help with phpMyAdmin, here are some people and places which will prove invaluable.

Official sites

- Homepage: `http://phpmyadmin.net`
- Manual and documentation: `http://phpmyadmin.net/documentation` (this contains the documentation for the latest development version; `Documentation.html` is the current documentation for your version and is included in the downloaded kit)
- Wiki: `http://wiki.phpmyadmin.net` contains information for both the users of phpMyAdmin and its developers
- Blog: `http://planet.phpmyadmin.net` aggregates the blogs of some phpMyAdmin developers
- Source code: phpMyAdmin is always offered in source code, but you'll find more information about the repositories at `http://www.phpmyadmin.net/home_page/improve.php`

Articles and tutorials

- Learning SQL using phpMyAdmin `http://www.php-editors.com/articles/sql_phpmyadmin.php`
- Doing more with phpMyAdmin (parts 1 and 2): `http://www.devshed.com/c/a/PHP/Doing-More-With-phpMyAdmin-Part-1`, `http://www.devshed.com/c/a/PHP/Doing-More-with-phpMyAdmin-Part-2`

Community

- Support home page: `http://www.phpmyadmin.net/home_page/support.php`
- Official mailing list: for users: `https://lists.sourceforge.net/lists/listinfo/phpmyadmin-users`;

  for developers of phpMyAdmin: `https://lists.sourceforge.net/lists/listinfo/phpmyadmin-devel`
- Official forums: `https://sourceforge.net/projects/phpmyadmin/forums/forum/72909`
- Official IRC channel: #phpmyadmin on `irc.freenode.net`
- Microblogging: `http://identi.ca/phpmyadmin`, the project's official microblogging site
- Facebook: `http://www.facebook.com/pages/PhpMyAdmin/157021164334486`
- Ohloh: The page `http://www.ohloh.net/p/phpmyadmin` tracks phpMyAdmin's progress in terms of the source code changes

Twitter

- Producers of the popular XAMPP system which includes phpMyAdmin: `http://twitter.com/#!/apachefriends`
- Quick news about phpMyAdmin: `http://twitter.com/#!/phpmya`
- For Open Source news: `http://twitter.com/PacktOpenSource`

Index

About the author

Marc Delisle was awarded "MySQL Community Member of the year 2009" because of his involvement with phpMyAdmin. He started to contribute to the project in December 1998, when he made the multi-language version. He is still involved with phpMyAdmin as a developer and project administrator.

Marc is a system administrator at Cegep de Sherbrooke, Québec, Canada. He has been teaching networking, security, and web application development. In one of his classes, he was pleased to meet a phpMyAdmin user from Argentina. Marc lives in Sherbrooke with his wife and they enjoy spending time with their four children.

About the Reviewer

Michal Čihař was born in 1980 in Prague, the capital city of the Czech Republic, and he is still living there. He studied Software Engineering at the Czech Technical University, and during these studies he started contributing to several free software projects, with the biggest contributions being made to phpMyAdmin and Gammu, and related projects. He currently works for SUSE, mostly on the SUSE Linux Enterprise platform.

Michal has been active in the phpMyAdmin project since 2001, when he started as a translator for the Czech language, later moving to a developer role (working, for example, on index manipulation, and export and import subsystems), and since 2010 he has also acted as a secondary project manager.

[PACKT] open source
PUBLISHING community experience distilled

Thank you for buying
phpMyAdmin Starter

About Packt Publishing

Packt, pronounced 'packed', published its first book "*Mastering phpMyAdmin for Effective MySQL Management*" in April 2004 and subsequently continued to specialize in publishing highly focused books on specific technologies and solutions.

Our books and publications share the experiences of your fellow IT professionals in adapting and customizing today's systems, applications, and frameworks. Our solution based books give you the knowledge and power to customize the software and technologies you're using to get the job done. Packt books are more specific and less general than the IT books you have seen in the past. Our unique business model allows us to bring you more focused information, giving you more of what you need to know, and less of what you don't.

Packt is a modern, yet unique publishing company, which focuses on producing quality, cutting-edge books for communities of developers, administrators, and newbies alike. For more information, please visit our website: `www.packtpub.com`.

About Packt Open Source

In 2010, Packt launched two new brands, Packt Open Source and Packt Enterprise, in order to continue its focus on specialization. This book is part of the Packt Open Source brand, home to books published on software built around Open Source licences, and offering information to anybody from advanced developers to budding web designers. The Open Source brand also runs Packt's Open Source Royalty Scheme, by which Packt gives a royalty to each Open Source project about whose software a book is sold.

Writing for Packt

We welcome all inquiries from people who are interested in authoring. Book proposals should be sent to author@packtpub.com. If your book idea is still at an early stage and you would like to discuss it first before writing a formal book proposal, contact us; one of our commissioning editors will get in touch with you.

We're not just looking for published authors; if you have strong technical skills but no writing experience, our experienced editors can help you develop a writing career, or simply get some additional reward for your expertise.

Made in the USA
Middletown, DE
20 March 2020

86930781R00024